GW00383908

THE CARE OF SADDLERY

CONTENTS

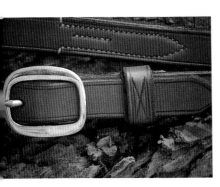

CLEANING

MATERIALS

The main materials required for cleaning saddlery are:
saddle soap, to wash and protect the leather;
metal polish, to put the shine back onto solid nickel and brass;
dandy brush, for removing hair and grease from felt pads, numnahs, material saddle linings and girths;
whitener, to freshen up pair web girths and leading reins for the show ring;
leather oil, ideal for the inside of three-fold girths and the flesh side of leather.

METHODS OF CLEANING

The safe working life of any piece of saddlery can easily be prolonged by regularly cleaning and feeding the leather.

With felt pads and saddles that have a linen or surge panel lining, brush any hairs off with a dandy brush.

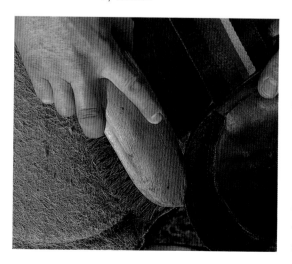

Linen-lined saddles can be cleaned by washing with a little soapy water to remove the build-up of dirt and sweat.

To avoid the sweat of an animal penetrating through a material lining and into the saddle flock, it is advisable to always use either a numnah or a saddle cloth.

Before any oil or saddle soap can be applied, both the top grain surface and the underneath flesh side of the leather must be free from any mud, dirt and animal sweat. If the leather is only lightly soiled, then a sponging with saddle soap should suffice. However, should the piece of saddlery be coated in mud, as is so often the case with leather girths, then it will need washing in a bucket of water and drying off.

Never leave any piece of saddlery on top of a fire or radiator to dry as the direct heat will cook and crack the leather. It is far better to remove all the excess water with a towel and then leave it in a warm room to dry naturally.

Once the leather is clean and dry, apply saddle soap with a damp sponge or rag to all surfaces. With those parts of saddlery that take a greater amount of wear, girth straps, girths and the ends of martingales, you may prefer to use a leather oil which will penetrate the thickness of the leather.

SAFETY CHECKS

During the routine cleaning of saddlery, make it a rule to always check over the leather and stitching, especially those parts which take most of the stress. This should become second nature and ensure that any weaknesses can be corrected beforehand, rather than break when in use.

SADDLES

CHECKING FOR A BROKEN TREE

There are several points on a saddle tree that are susceptible to breaking.

A Arch
B Laterals
C Cantle
D Stirrup bar mountings
E Tree points

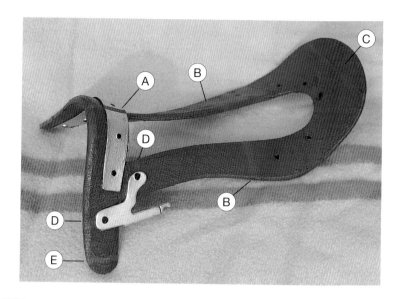

AUTHOR'S NOTE

In my experience there are certain saddles that can exhibit signs of a broken tree, i.e. they easily flex more than one inch and yet, when stripped down, the tree is sound although very flexible. In these cases a thorough restuffing can stiffen the saddle quite considerably.

When inspecting a saddle for soundness, the following points should be tested in turn.

1. To test the arch, rest the saddle against your stomach and, gripping each side of the pommel, try to move the front of the saddle up and down. Except for the flexible points, there should not be any movement or sound whatsoever.

2. While the saddle is in the same position, hold it in the middle of the arch and pull it towards you. If it is a rigid tree there should be absolutely no movement. With a spring tree there will be a certain amount of springing movement, approximately one inch or a little more, but with no creaking noises. The 'give' should be even; any saddle that gives more to one side than the other should be viewed with suspicion.

3. Ensure that there is no play in the cantle of the saddle.

4. Inspect the stirrup bars on each side for any signs of movement. The short thumb piece should be in a downward position and not seized in the upright position.

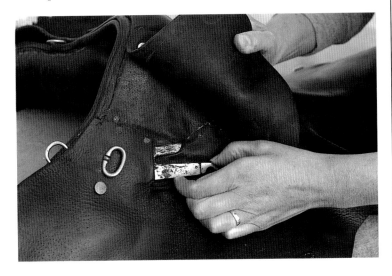

SAFETY CHECKS

Do not continue to use a saddle which you believe may have a broken tree. If either of points A or B (on the tree illus.) are broken, then the rider's weight will not be evenly distributed along the animal's back, whereas if the bars are loose, the stirrup leathers could easily fall off. Continuing to use a saddle with a broken cantle could result in the slackening off of the lateral webs in the seat of the saddle. If in any doubt - get it checked!

MAIN POINTS OF WEAR

The main points of wear on a saddle are shown in the diagram and are:

A   Pommel
B   Waist
C   Cantle
D   Lacing at back
E   Knee pads
F   Girth straps
G   Panel ends
H   Knee rolls
I   Stitching on girth straps
J   Tree points
K   Channel
L   Front lacing

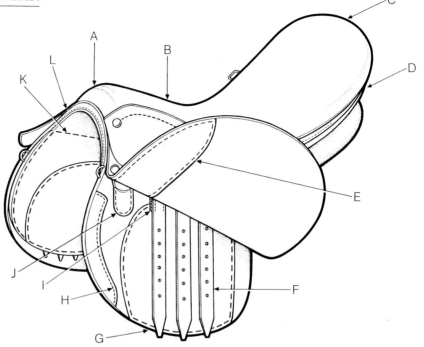

AVOIDING THE NEED FOR REPAIR

Illustrated here are a few tips which should help to avoid the need for unnecessary repairs on a saddle.

Buckle guards can greatly reduce the amount of wear that is put upon the saddle flaps by the girth buckles. By using guards made from as thin a leather as possible, it will reduce the bulk between the rider's legs and the horse.

Always oil the back and the front of the stitching on the girth straps and so reduce friction.

Likewise, always pay special attention when cleaning a saddle to the five to six inches of stitching across which the girth lies.

SADDLE STORAGE

After use, saddles are best kept on a purpose-made saddle stand or rack. These racks can either be free-standing, or else attached to a wall.

It is always better, whenever possible, to store only one saddle on each rack. There are two reasons for this. Firstly, the underneath of the panel needs to dry out and have air freely circulating around it after use. Secondly, it is possible for the extra saddles to put undue weight on the saddle at the bottom and cause the tubular supports of the rack to form indentations in that saddle's panel.

Saddles should always be carried supported, and *never* by the end of the flap as shown here. A saddle flap is only held into place at the back by six or seven nails and these can easily work loose if a saddle is carried this way.

When resting a saddle against a stone wall, always fold the girth, of whatever material or type, over the seat to protect the cantle. Once the edge of the saddle seat has been damaged at the cantle, it will usually require either an unsightly patch or an expensive repair to put matters right.

BREASTPLATE FITTINGS

If you use a breastplate, it should always be fastened to a dee or staple that is secured through the saddle tree. The small dees which are held into place with a piece of thin leather have insufficient strength for the stress put upon a breastplate.

SYNTHETIC SADDLES

There is a new breed of saddles made from Cordura and other synthetic materials. These saddles have the advantages of being lightweight and easy to clean. A warm soapy sponge is all that is needed to remove sweat and mud from the fabric, and any kind of oiling is not recommended.

Saddles which use a knitted nylon material on the panel are best used with a saddle cloth or numnah. The makers advise the use of their own synthetic range of accessories with these saddles as oiled stirrup leathers can spoil the material on the flaps.

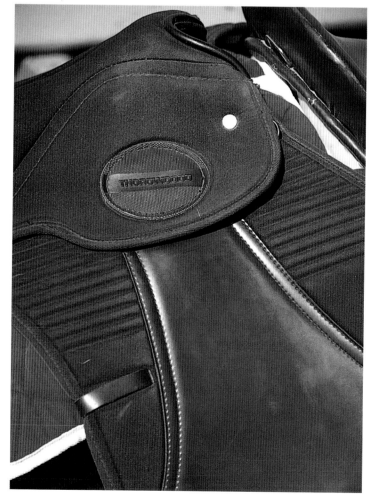

GIRTHS AND STIRRUP LEATHERS

To ensure that a three-fold girth remains supple, check that there is a length of material inside the girth and keep it well oiled. If there is no such piece of material, it is a straightforward task to cut a strip three inches wide from heavy cotton, canvas or from an old woollen blanket to fit inside the girth.

Material girths such as those made from lampwick, tubular or race web should be regularly washed to remove the animal's salty sweat deposits. If they have leather fittings, take care to keep these as dry as possible. An advantage with nylon web fittings is that the girth is machine washable.

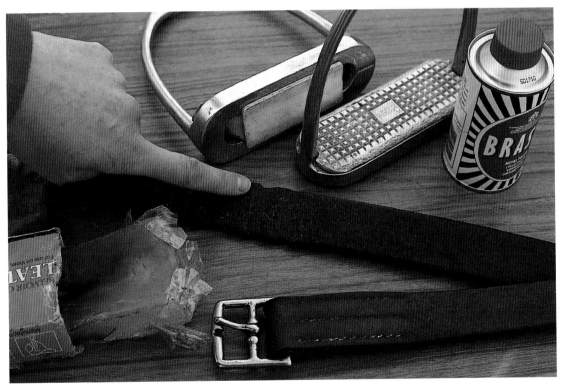

Stirrup leathers need constant attention, both in oiling and checking for wear. Pay particular attention to the parts that take the pressure of the irons and the bars of the saddle tree. If they require restitching at any time, consider if it is worth shortening them by two or three inches. This will have the effect of moving the points of wear caused by the buckle tongue and the stirrup iron to another part of the leather, an important consideration if the leathers are always used on the same hole.

BRIDLEWORK

MAIN POINTS OF WEAR

The illustration indicates the parts of a bridle which, in my own workshop experience, are those most commonly requiring attention and repair.

REDUCING WEAR

Always make it a habit to unfasten billet returns before cleaning and oiling. The flesh or underside of the leather is in constant contact with the bit and must receive special attention.

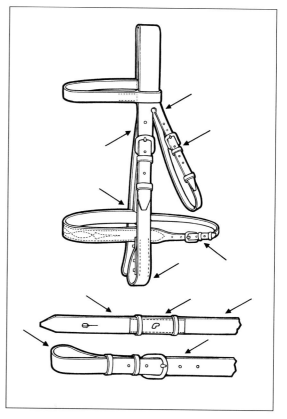

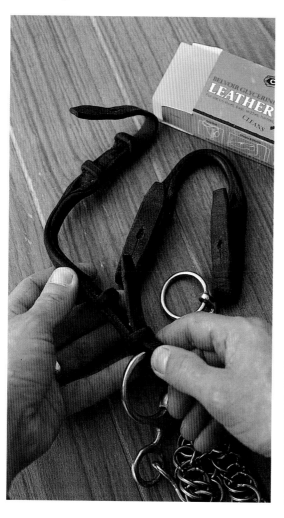

SAFETY CHECKS

Regularly check for any worn slots in the mouthpieces of bits. Flat, loose ring snaffle rings are prone to wearing sharp edges on the mouthpiece, especially if the bit is made from the softer nickel alloy metal.

In addition to oiling the outside surfaces of the leather, a considerable amount of wear can be prevented by feeding a little oil inside the buckle returns. Likewise, a few drops of oil dribbled down the hook studs into the platforms which hold them onto the rein and bridle cheeks will pay dividends.

Always make sure that there is a small hole punched into the leather at the point where the cheek point and the throat part of the head piece divide. If there is not a hole there already, it is a simple job to insert one using a revolving hole punch. The hole will greatly reduce the chances of the head piece splitting at this point.

SAFETY CHECKS

When using a running martingale, always use rein stops to prevent the martingale rings being caught up onto the hook studs of the rein billet. Pay special attention when cleaning to the 12 inches or so of the rein along which the martingale rings slide. Constant use with a tight martingale can drastically weaken the reins at this point.

THE SHOW RING

Saddlery should always be used in a clean and tidy condition but the show ring is the place where it should always be *par excellence.*

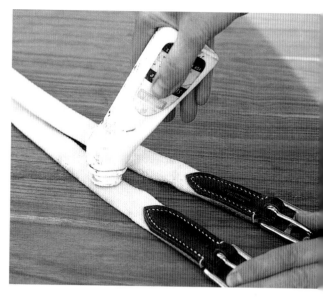

WEB GIRTHS AND LEADS

Show girth   Narrow, white, pair-web girths can be refreshed between shows with an application of shoe whitener.

Web leading reins   These can be treated in the same way but, be warned, in wet weather the shoe whitener is liable to come off on your hands.

CLEANING BITS, ROSETTES AND BROWBANDS

Bits   Metal polish can add that extra sparkle to the cheekpieces of a bit, do however make certain to wash the mouthpiece after cleaning to remove any unpleasant tasting cleaner.

Metal rosettes and browbands   Use a tooth brush to thoroughly polish any fancy centre pieces on a rosette. Clincher or chain-link browbands should have an application of metal polish, taking care not to get any on the leather as it tends to dry out into a white powder.

PLAITING BROWBANDS

Any plain leather browband can be made into something special by covering it in cotton or velvet ribbon.

Select two lengths of material and stitch them together at one end, leaving two inches to form a tail, then place the browband between the two ribbons so as to cover up the stitching.

Bring each ribbon in turn over the face of the browband. As each ribbon passes across the leather, lift the other so that half the ribbon will be covered, thus producing a V pattern.

Finish off by stitching the ribbons together as close to the browband as possible and leave a tail to match the other end.

There are countless variations in browband design in both choice of material and plaiting techniques.

Pay special attention when cleaning material browbands as warm water may cause the dye in the leather to run, so discolouring the ribbon.

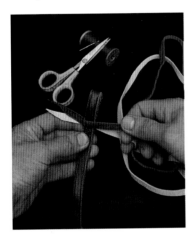

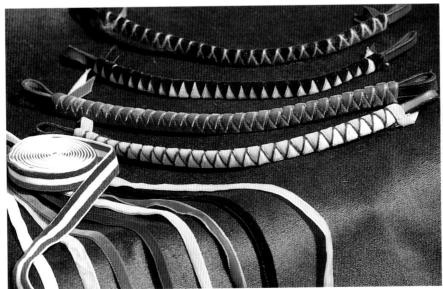

TOOLS FOR BASIC REPAIRS

Many repairs can be successfully carried out using only the most elementary selection of tools as shown here. They are from left to right:

nail claw; revolving punch; hammer; awl, straight blade; awl, curved blade; thread; beeswax; needles; scissors; pliers; knife

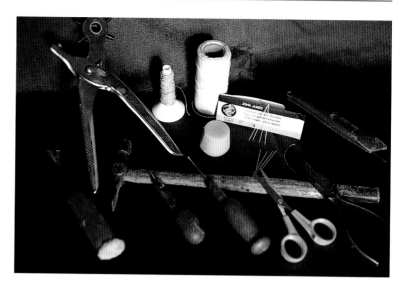

There are many tasks, mainly on saddles, that can be completed without the need for a pair of stitching clamps. You will find, however, that when stitching bridlework, a pair of clamps approximately 33 inches high is invaluable.

MAKING A CURVED NEEDLE

To restitch the back of the panel to the saddle you will need a curved awl and needle. These needles can be bought ready made or can easily be made by heating an ordinary needle until red hot and tapping it to shape with a hammer.

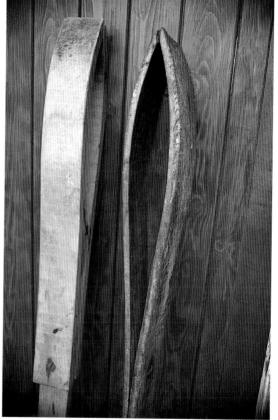

The addresses of suppliers of specialist saddlery tools can be found on page 23.

HAND-STITCHING TECHNIQUE

THREAD

Although proprietary threads available in large spools can be bought for hand stitching, ordinary plaiting thread is exactly the same in make up and is ideal for repairing bridlework and for the finer stitching on saddles such as the knee pads. The heavier jobs such as restitching stirrup leathers, girth straps and panel ends should be carried out using either a special 18/5 or 18/6 thread or else by using double thickness plaiting thread.

Before starting any stitching, the first task should always be to wax your thread. This is simply done by pulling the cut length of thread through a block of beeswax.

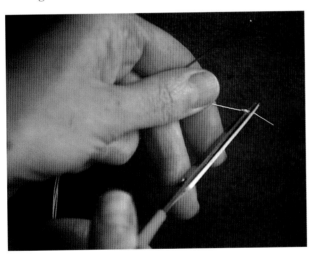

The next step is to thread the needles. **Single-needle stitching** requires only one needle with a knot tied at one end. Once tied, cut the tail of the thread as close to the knot as possible.

Double-needle stitching is slightly more complicated as you need to work with a needle at each end of the thread. With the needles threaded, the returns must be adjusted until they match.

SINGLE-NEEDLE STITCHING

Start by placing the work to be stitched into the clamps with the stitch marks on the right-hand side.

NOTE: **left-handed people should reverse all instructions.**

The next step is to insert the awl into the second stitch mark from the end furthest away from you and bring the needle through from the left-hand side.

To make the stitch, return the needle back to the left-hand side via the furthermost stitch hole. On this first stitch you may have to first align the holes with the awl.

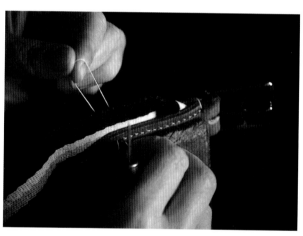

Continue along the length of the piece of work, in this case the buckle chape on a web girth, each time bringing the needle through from the left- to the right-hand side and then back again. Each time lift the larger stitch at the back of the work over the top of the returning needle.

When the stitching is complete, finish off by tying a knot at the back of the work as close to the stitching as possible.

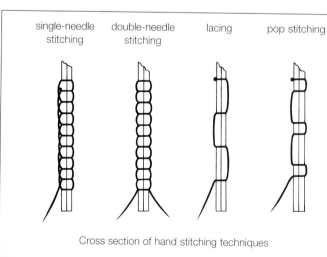

single-needle stitching   double-needle stitching   lacing   pop stitching

Cross section of hand stitching techniques

- **Single-needle stitching** Suitable for: rug fittings, webbing girths, girth straps, bridle buckles, knee grips on saddles.
- **Double-needle stitching** Suitable for: stirrup leathers, leather girths, saddle panels, rein billets.
- **Lacing** (with curved needle) Suitable for: pulling up the back of the saddle, re-covering the panel on the saddle, knee rolls on certain saddles.
- **Pop stitching** Suitable for: pulling up the front of the saddle, re-covering the panel on the saddle, quilting material panel on the saddle.

DOUBLE-NEEDLE STITCHING

Wax a length of thread and thread a needle onto each end. Start the stitching by putting a needle through the second hole from the end and pull it through until there are equal amounts of thread on each side of the work.

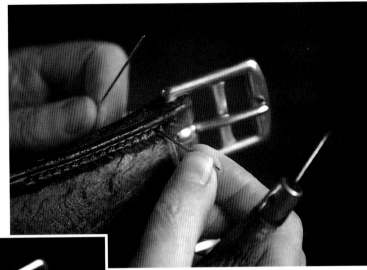

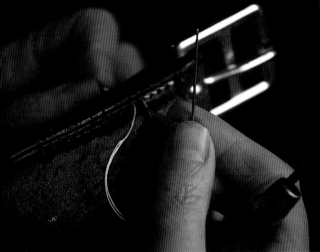

Bring the left-hand needle through to the right-hand side and return the other needle from the right- to the left-hand side. The two needles are then pulled firmly to form an equal-sized stitch on each side of the work.

Continue stitching in this way to the end of the repair when you will then need to restitch over the last three stitches before cutting the thread off at the back of the work. This way there is no need to tie any knots when finishing off.

SAFETY CHECK

Whenever you are restitching stirrup leathers, *never* stitch only the last two or three stitches at the end. This is a dangerous practice because, although the other stitches may not have broken, the chances are that they will have worn. *Always* renew the entire length of stitching. On no account should a stirrup leather ever be spliced along its length. If it shows signs of wear, there is no option but to replace them completely.

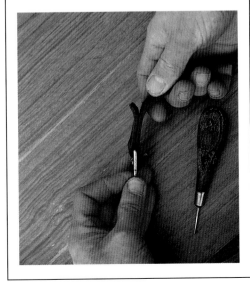

REPAIRING SADDLES AND BRIDLEWORK

To get used to the feel of a needle, awl and thread in your hands, start on something straightforward; once you have gained experience and confidence you can progress to more adventurous repairs.

Knee pads on saddle flaps are an ideal starting point, especially as they do not require a pair of stitching clamps to hold them.

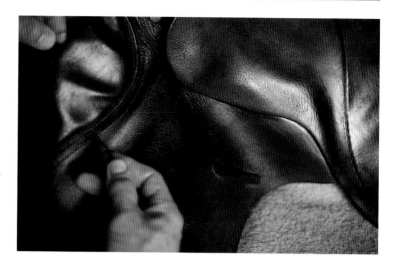

Likewise the **ends of a panel** are an uncomplicated repair and always seem to wear where the girth lies over the stitching no matter how well it is oiled.

Girth chapes, although requiring stitching clamps, offer not too difficult an opportunity to the novice as there are no loops involved.

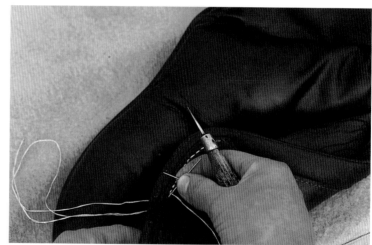

SAFETY CHECK

Whenever you have finished any stitching which is likely to come into contact with the horse, always check that there are no sharp knots or stitching standing proud that could rub against the horse. Any rough or uneven parts should be levelled off with a wide-faced hammer.

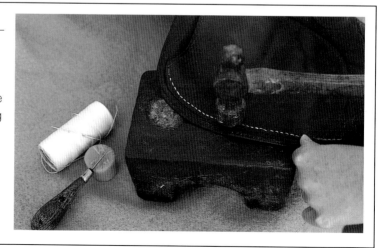

RESTITCHING GIRTH STRAPS

To restitch the girth straps on a saddle it will be necessary to drop the front of the panel to gain access to where they are stitched onto the tree webs.

AUTHOR'S NOTE

While this photograph and the photograph on page 14 illustrate a Stanley knife, in a fully equipped workshop, a saddler would normally use a half round, or head, knife when dropping the front or the back of a saddle.

Cut the large stitches holding the panel to the flaps and the top part of the saddle and remove the points of the saddle tree from their pockets. On a few saddles you may find that nails have been used either instead of or as well as stitching.

You should now find that you have access to the ends of the tree webs to which the girth straps are attached. To restitch the girth straps, use a well-waxed, double thickness thread and a single needle. First remove all the old stitches and, as with stirrup leathers, always renew the stitching completely, *never* just the end stitches.

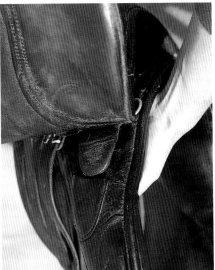

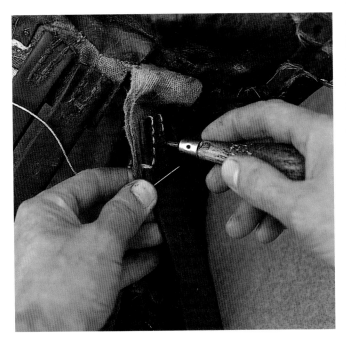

SAFETY CHECKS

When attaching the girth, always use the strap nearest to the front of the saddle plus one of the other two straps. The front girth strap should always be stitched onto a separate tree web so that in the event of one of the webs breaking, the girth will remain held in place by the other tree web.

PULLING UP THE FRONT OF A SADDLE

Gently ease the tree points back into their pockets and position the panel tightly up against the top of the saddle. Before com-mencing to restitch the front, make sure that you have first centralized the panel equidistant to the middle of the arch.

To pull up, use the same thread as for restitching the girth straps and follow the old stitch holes around the front of the saddle. Make sure that the knots you tie in the thread to start and to finish the stitch-ing are not where they can come into con-tact with, and rub, the horse.

SAFETY CHECKS

It is totally incorrect and unsafe to nail the front of the panel to the saddle tree. Should a nail work loose, dislodge and come into contact with the horse's back, the result could be calamitous.

PULLING UP THE BACK OF A SADDLE

Thread a curved needle with the thickest thread to hand, double it over so that it may be used double thickness, and tie a large knot at one end. This knot should be positioned between the panel and the top part of the saddle as can be seen in this picture.

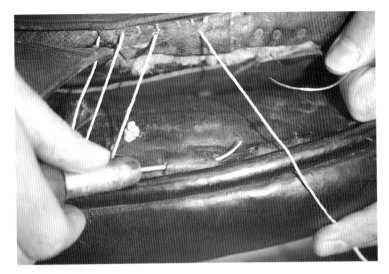

Unlike any other stitching previously covered, the long lacing stitches are first put into place with a curved needle and awl and left loose.

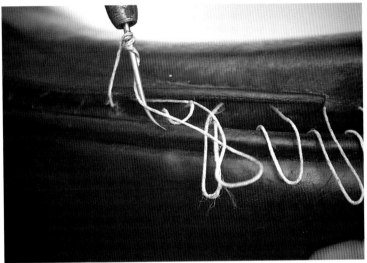

Once all of the stitches are in place, they are then tensioned up with a curved awl and finished off with a large knot which is tucked away between the panel and the saddle top.

It is sometimes necessary because of worn leather inside the panel and below the saddle seat to put a small stitch to secure the panel, flap and skirt together at the beginning and the end of the stitching.

LOOPS

Having got to grips with straightforward stitching, the next step is to tackle restitching loops. Try not to start with anything too fine such as those on a bridle throatlash.

If you are restitching old loops, then the stitch holes should guide you as to how far the loops need to be inserted between the two thicknesses of leather. If you are using a new piece of leather instead, do not insert the loop more than halfway inside the width of the strap.

Work along the line of the stitching on the first side of the loop, cross the thread over and stitch along the second side until you reach the position where the other end of the loop is to fit in. Complete one stitch on the far side of the loop, and the other stitches from the side nearest to you.

Take great care when stitching loops into place, not to use the awl blade to lever them into position as it is all too easy to snap an awl blade in this way. Once the end of the loop is in position between the leather, ease the loop over so that the awl has a straight line to work along.

AUTHOR'S NOTE

Throughout this book, I have dealt with repairs that do not require any new leather. When repairing loops however, it is often necessary to use a new piece of loop material. In most homes and yards there are often old items of leather such as defunct boots or saddlery that could be pressed into service as a source of loop material.

SUPPLIERS OF TOOLS AND MATERIALS

Craftwares Ltd., Home Farm, Hotham, York, YO4 3UN. Tel. 01430 423636

J.T. Batchelor Ltd., 9-10 Culford Mews, London, N1 4DZ. Tel. 0171 254 2962/8521

Le Prevo Leather, Blackfriars, Stowell Street, Newcastle upon Tyne, NE1 4XN. Tel. 0191 261 7648

Thorowgood, The Saddlery, Fryers Road, Bloxwich, Walsall, W. Midlands, WS3 2XJ. Tel. 01922 711676

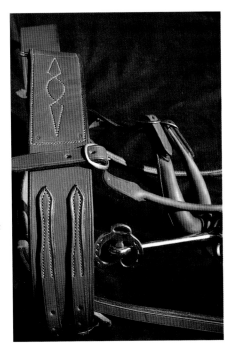

The leading makers of synthetic saddles, they provide replacement girth straps through saddlery stockists. However, if there is difficulty in obtaining replacements, they can be contacted direct.

In addition to the above firms, several repair items used in this book can be found in most large towns.

Needles   Blunt-ended needles can be bought from camping and needlework shops, and saddlery shops where they are sold for plaiting.

Thread   Carpet and plaiting thread is ideal.

Beeswax   Chemists, honey farms, health food shops, hardware and craft shops will often sell blocks of beeswax.

OTHER BOOKS BY SAME AUTHOR

REPAIR YOUR OWN SADDLERY AND HARNESS

BRIDLEWORK

CARE & REPAIR OF RUGS

All published by J. A. Allen, London.

British Library Cataloguing-in-Publication Data.
A catalogue record for this book is available from the
British Library

ISBN 0.85131.689.1

Published in Great Britain in 1997 by
J. A. Allen & Company Limited,
1 Lower Grosvenor Place, Buckingham Palace Road,
London, SW1W OEL

Design and Typesetting by Paul Saunders
Series editor Jane Lake
Printed in Hong Kong by Dah Hua Printing Press Co. Ltd.